Comune di Roma
Assessorato alle Politiche Culturali

Sovraintendenza ai Beni Culturali

THE CAPITOLINE MUSEUMS
MUSEUMS
SHORT GUIDE

 Electa

Cover
Mosaic of the Doves,
detail

Traslation
Darius Arya

Comune di Roma
Assessorato alle Politiche
Culturali

Gianni Borgna
Assessore

Sovraintendenza ai Beni
Culturali

Eugenio La Rocca
Sovraintendente

Anna Mura Sommella
*Dirigente dei Musei
di Arte Antica*

Maria Elisa Tittoni
*Dirigente dei Musei
di Arte Medioevale
e Moderna*

Texts by
Nunzio Giustozzi
with the collaboration of
Perla Innocenti

Photographs
Archivio dei Musei
Capitolini

Editorial project by Electa, Milan
Elemond Editori Associati

www.electaweb.it

CONTENTS

THE CAMPIDOGLIO

The Campidoglio is a museum of extraordinary historic
and cultural value. It is composed of the square,
the buildings and the archaeological and historic-artistic
collections. Recently, due to the recent opening
of the subterranean passageway, the most important
ancient monuments also have become part
of the Campidoglio. The area also offers spectacular
views of pagan and Christian Rome. The perfection,
the sense of magical harmony achieved
by the monumental flight of steps is not just the fruit
of Michelangelo's marvellous architectural design.
The layout of the piazza, which is enclosed by buildings
but opens up like a stage toward the city, is above
all the outcome of its millenary history during which the
hill of the Campidoglio represented the religious
and political center of Rome.

Piazza del Campidoglio (Capitoline Square)

In Antiquity

Even though an ancient tradition derives the name "Campidoglio" from the discovery of a skull (*caput*) when the foundations of the Temple of Jupiter Capitolinus were laid, it seems that *Capitolium* means "dominant rise." In fact, originally two wooded rises, the *Arx* and the *Capitolium*, separated by a small valley, constituted the hill. The small valley housed the *Asylum* i.e., the area that Romulus opened to the inhabitants of the neighboring villages to augment the population of the young town. Indeed, recent archaeological surveys demonstrated the veracity of the legends about the origins of Rome and the myth of its foundation. Traces of an even older presence on the hill were found near the Palazzo dei Conservatori (The Conservators' Palace). The material is dated as early as the end of the Bronze Age (1200-1000 BC). Some infant burials and the remains of metal handicraft constitute the findings of this early settlement. The definitive consecration of the *Capitolium* is the work of the last kings of Rome. In fact, the Tarquins ordered the construction of the Temple of Jupiter *Optimus Maximus*. It was dedicated to the Capitoline Triad (Jupiter, Juno, and Minerva) venerated in the three *cellæ* of the building. The sources report that magnificent decorations enriched the monument. The massive foundations of the temple are perfectly preserved, enveloped within the structures of the 16th-century Palazzo Caffarelli. The sanctuary, dedicated in the first year of the Republican period (509 BC), became the symbol of Roman civilization. It was replicated in all the new

Jacques Carlu, *View of the Capitolium dominated by the Temple of Jupiter Capitolinus* (1924)

cities that Rome founded, and it was the final destination of triumphal ceremonies. In fact, it was customary that the victorious generals who came back from successful campaigns marched in a parade in the city through the *Via Sacra* (Sacred Street), followed by prisoners and war spoils, to arrive at the *Capitolium* to make sacrifices.

The other Capitoline rise, with its rocky slopes solidly fortified, was the acropolis (*arx*) of the city. On it, where the massive Church of Santa Maria in Aracœli currently stands out, once stood the Temple of Juno *Moneta*. Because the temple was easily defendable, the premises of the public mint were located there.

In the 78 BC, the slopes of the *Capitolium* facing the Forum were regularized through the construction of the majestic structures of the *Tabularium*, the archives in which the Roman State preserved thousands of documents and law texts. When the building was erected, the Romans left untouched the small pre-existing (196 BC) sanctuary of Veiovis (the adolescent Jupiter), a mysterious Italic divinity with ties to the underworld and protector of the marginalized. The divinity was very popular during the Republican age. In this period, numerous monuments (small temples, altars, porticoes, statues and honorary arches, trophies, fountains, etc.) enriched the piazza that surrounded the Temple of Jupiter (the Capitoline Area). In fact, intent on promoting their ideological propaganda, the most important families of the Roman aristocracy commissioned the most famous artists of the day.

From the Middle Ages to the Renaissance
In the Middle Ages, the architectural structures fell into ruin or were destroyed in order to recuperate construction materials. The marbles were burnt in the furnaces to obtain lime. We can find an echo of the ancient grandiosity—already weakened by devastation and calamities as well as by the intervention of the last emperors who despoiled Rome to decorate Constantinople—through the description of the *Mirabilia Urbis* (The Wonders of Rome), true Medieval tourist guides. Whereas the remains of the Temple of Jupiter ironically became pastures for goats (*Monte Caprino*), in the XI century the still massive remains of the *Tabularium* witnessed the strengthening of powerful baronial families always competing for supremacy.
Later, in 1143, with the birth of the Roman Com-

mune, the Senators became responsible for the government of the city after an antipapal revolution. They occupied the building, which became named after them. In fact, the sixteenth century façade hides the heavily fortified crenellated towers, visible on the sides, which strengthen the corners of the fortress (14th-15th century). The fortress became the center of urban life, even though, by then, its location was outside the populated areas. The *Palazzo Senatorio* (The Senator Palace), which today is still the site of the municipality, possessed a tower (damaged and reconstructed in a central location in the 16th century) which housed a bell (the "patarina") used to call the population to gather. The Romans had taken the bell from the people of Viterbo after a battle in 1200. It was substituted only at the beginning of the 19th century. The construction of the *loggia* overlooking the square where the market took place created an important change. Whereas in the Roman period the main monuments of the hill were oriented toward the Forum, in the Middle Ages the Campidoglio opens toward *Campus Martius* (Field of Mars).

In 1363, the first statutes of the citizens determined that only one foreign Senator was paired with three elective magistrates, the Conservators, the representatives of the new social class, that recently had obtained power, in charge of the administration of the city. Therefore, the transformation of the pre-existing buildings into the magnificent site of the *Palazzo dei Conservatori* took place in that period. The building, which had a portico on the ground floor and Guelph cross-windows on the first floor,

Palazzo dei Conservatori, Hall of the Eagles: representation of games conducted on the Capitoline piazza

housed from the very beginning the antiquities collection of the Campidoglio.

Until the fifteenth century the cohabitation of the communal institutions with the papacy was not always peaceful. In 1471, with a skillful political plan, Pope Sixtus IV gave as a present to the Roman population the "renowned bronze statues" which until then had been housed in the Lateran. The transferal of the sculptures, which represented the continuity between ancient Rome and the temporal power of the papacy, was intended to confirm the predominance of the Church over the civic autonomy. The liberal act of donating the *She-Wolf* elevated the Campidoglio to a place a memory. The *She-wolf*, made complete through the addition of the twins and displayed on the façade of the Palazzo dei Conservatori, became the symbol of the city.

The Piazza: an Experiment in Perfection
In 1536, in order to embellish the Campidoglio for the arrival of the emperor Charles V, Pope Paul III Farnese entrusted to Michelangelo the task of conferring an architectural unity to the diversity of the Capitoline building complex. The next two years witnessed the formulation of a brilliant project according to which Michelangelo decided to place the equestrian statue of Marcus Aurelius in the square. For this purpose, the statue was transferred from the Lateran and placed in the center of a magnificent star-shaped pavement design. The pavement was known through an engraving. However, it was only constructed in 1940. Currently, a faithful copy of the statue substitutes the original. Miche-

10

Anonymous drawing made in the middle of the 16th century, the Capitoline "stage"

langelo's designs began to take shape only in the successive decades, particularly through the work of Giacomo Della Porta. Michelangelo's project was concluded more than a century after its creation with the completion of the *Palazzo Nuovo* (New Palace), on the left side of the piazza. The building was constructed in order to mirror the Palazzo dei Conservatori and add symmetry to the entire piazza. The equilibrium of the complex has also been achieved by using the giant order, characterized by massive cornices and decorative balconies adorned with statues, on all of the three buildings. The relationship between the empty spaces and the constructed ones as well as the harmonious use of col-

or, decorations, and friezes (whose splendor has been exalted by a recent and accurate restoration) are balanced. Palazzo Senatorio was the first building renewed with the construction of a double staircase placed at the entrance of the main, upper, "noble" floor. This was the only change that Michelangelo saw. With the arrival of the *Acqua Felice* aqueduct, a double basin fountain with Greek marble veneer was created to flank each flight of steps. Two statues of river gods originally from the Baths of Constantine on the Quirinal but already present in the Campidoglio were placed on both sides of the fountain. On the left side, the *Nile* leans on the sphinx and holds the cornucopia of fertility and abundance. On the right, the *Tiber* group is represented and, for the glory of Rome, a tiger has been transformed into a She-wolf. Finally, a statue of Minerva (too small for the setting) was placed in the spacious central niche. The goddess is sitting and is dressed in porphyry (a very prestigious purple stone). It was restored as *Triumphant Roma* through the addition of the attributes of the goddess. The façade of the Palazzo Senatorio represents the dramatic culmination of a route that begins from the slightly graded ramp whose balustrade acquired important sculptures over the years. The sculptures include the Egyptian lions transformed into fountains placed at the foot of the hill, and the *Dioscuri* reconstructed at the top of the ramp. The sons of Zeus, rushed to Rome to announce the victory of Rome over the other Latin people in the battle at Lake Regillus (499 or 496 BC) and watered their horses at the spring of the nymph Juturna in the Forum.

Colossal statue
of one of the Dioscuri
on the balustrade
of the Capitoline piazza

THE EXTENSIVE HISTORY
OF THE CAPITOLINE MUSEUMS

Courtyard of the Palazzo dei Conservatori
with fragments of the colossal statue
of Constantine

The Growth and Arrangement of the Collections

The growth of the Capitoline collections took place over more than five centuries and represents the most significant moments of Roman history, from the Renaissance to the modern age. The creation of the Capitoline Museums is framed in the cultural context of the 15th century was not only considered in terms of its function for potential reuse, but also as the object of the antiquarian and collectors' interest.

15th–16th Century

A commemorative inscription located at the entrance of the Palazzo dei Conservatori records that, in 1471, Pope Sixtus IV restituted four ancient bronze statues to the Roman People: the *She-wolf*, the *colossal head of Constantine* (with the hand and globe), the *Spinario* (the boy pulling out a thorn

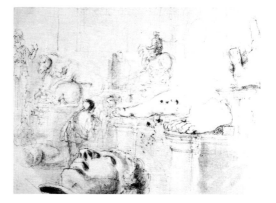

from his foot), and the so-called *Gypsy*. The four statues represent the beginning of the first public collection of antiquity. The Pope's political-ideological gesture thus marks the beginning of the continual flow of important and always more numerous ancient sculptures to the Campidoglio. The Conservators themselves purchased the gilded bronze statue of Hercules in order to make it a "monument to the glory of Rome." The statue was found during the papacy of Sixtus IV in the proximity of the church of Santa Maria in Cosmedin. A few years later, the remains of the colossal statue of Constantine (found in 1486 in the Basilica of Maxentius) were placed in the Palazzo dei Conservatori.

These works were added to the few existing ones that had been placed on the hill during the mediaeval period. All of them were closely related to the functional aspects of the civic premises. These pieces included the marble group depicting a lion attacking a horse and funerary urns. Originally, the marble group was located at the top of the staircase of the Palazzo Senatorio where capital punishments were announced and sometimes executed. The funerary urns, reutilized in the Capitoline market as measures for grain and salt, came from the Mausoleum of Augustus. The inscriptions that Cola di Rienzo gathered on the Campidoglio in the first half of the 14th century constituted the first civic collections. It seems that until the middle of the 16th century a strong historic connotation characterized them. Indeed, the objects were chosen according to their historical significance rather than their intrinsic artistic value. In this sense, as previously mentioned, the addition of the twins to the *She-Wolf* was intended to erase the ominous character of the symbol of justice that the statue had assumed when it was located in the Lateran. Indeed, such an addition was now meant to underline the benevolent character of *Mater Romanorum* (Mother of the Romans), emblem of the city, in substitution of the lion. In 1515, the three historical reliefs pertaining to a celebratory monument erected in honor of Marcus Aurelius, found in the church of Saints Luca and Martina in the Forum, were transferred to the Palazzo dei Conservatori. They represented the ideal continuity between the ancient world and the Renaissance Campidoglio through the depiction of the submission of the barbarians and the triumph and sacrifice before the Temple of Capitoline Jupiter.

In 1538, due to the firm will of Paul III, the equestrian statue of Marcus Aurelius was transferred from the Lateran to the Campidoglio. It had escaped the systematic melting down of ancient bronze statues because it had been identified in the medieval period as Constantine, the first Christian emperor. In addition, in 1541, Paul III donated a large statue of Athena, which decorated the central niche of the staircase of the Palazzo Senatorio. Today, it is located in the atrium of Palazzo Nuovo. In fact, a new arrangement of the sculptures and inscriptions housed in the palace followed Michelangelo's architectural interventions in the Capitoline piazza.

By the second half of the fifteenth century, the fol-

lowing diverse and important acquisitions included the *Consular Fasti*, the so-called *Capitoline
Brutus*, and the tablets with the *Lex de imperio
Vespasiani* (the law from the reign of Vespasian)—
almost a Decalogue, in the popular meaning,
against wrongdoing. These acquisitions respect the
original historical nature of the collection. Such
continuity was interrupted in 1566 when Pius V
wanting "to purge the Vatican of pagan idols,"
decided to transfer to the Campidoglio a series of
works whose exquisite artistic character ushered in
the birth of a true museum of ancient art.

Jeronymus Cock,
The Capitoline piazza
(1562)

17th-18th century

Even though in the 17th century the growth of the
collection slowed due to the competition with the
private antiquarian market, the overcrowding of
the spaces occupied by the statues in the Palazzo
dei Conservatori rendered even the regular execution of the ancient civic magistrate functions difficult. Indeed, the magistrates used those environments as offices and public spaces. Therefore,
already at the end of the 16th century the transferal of the sculptures to the Palazzo Nuovo had
begun. Carlo Rainaldi completed the construction
of this palace in 1654. However, the building was
used as a museum only in 1733 with Clement XII's
purchase of the extraordinary collection of busts of
famous men, emperors, and philosophers that previously had belonged to Cardinal Albani. The purchase was possible due to the lottery held at the
Piazza del Campidoglio. After the inauguration of
the museum in 1734, according to a project focused

on the protection and valorization of the artistic and archaeological patrimony of the State of the Church, Clement XII himself and Benedict fourteenth made further donations. Masterpieces such as the so-called *Dying Gladiator*, the *Capitoline Venus*, and the *Eros and Psyche* group enriched the rooms of the museum. The fragments of the *Forma Urbis Romae* (the marble plan of the city, dating to the Severan age, discovered in the 16th century in the area of the Forum of Peace) were arranged along the monumental staircase where they remained until the beginning of the last century.

The two *Centaurs* located in the middle of the Large Hall and the *Mosaic of the Doves* (made of minute tesserae) number among the last prestigious purchases that took place in the second half of the 18th century. They, as well as the *Faun* made in *rosso antico* marble, came from Hadrian's Villa near Tivoli. The arrangement of this extraordinary collection of ancient sculptures in Palazzo Nuovo makes the Capitoline Museum an exceptional testimony of the eighteenth century museological conception, which favored a disposition of the pieces according to categories and a refined display of the works of art. In the last two hundred and fifty years the arrangement of the works of art did not substantially change, as it appears evident from the drawings of the 18th and 19th centuries. The peculiarity of the restoration schools, which determined the reconstruction and interpretation of the ancient sculptures represents a considerable document of the cultivated collecting of the past centuries as well.

Great Hall of Palazzo Nuovo

The typological diversification of the Capitoline Museums took place in 1749 with Benedict XIV's creation of the Picture Gallery in order to encourage further study of the paintings and avoid the dispersion of two famous private collections of that period: the Sacchetti and the Pio di Savoia's.

When in 1771 the Pio Clementino Museum was created in the Vatican, the growth of the archaeological donations to the Capitoline Museums stopped. From that moment on, the popes directed their entire attention to their new museum.

19th–20th Century

The revolutionary and Napoleonic vicissitudes affected the Campidoglio. Indeed, some of its masterpieces were transferred to France. The tenacious good offices of Canova (director of the museum at that time) partially recuperated some works of art after Napoleon's fall.

In 1838, the Capitoline Museum was given back to the Conservators. In exchange for the restitution, the museum had to give up its rich collection of Egyptian works of art. They were moved to the Vatican. The Castellani (mostly Greek and Etruscan-Italic vases, including the famous *Crater of Aristonothos*), and Cini (porcelain pieces that were added to painting gallery) donations, as well as the creation of the Capitoline collection of medals were the relevant events that took place on the eve of the proclamation of Rome as the Capital of Italy (1870).

The feverish building activity and the subsequent excavations that took place in order to provide the city with public buildings and residential neighborhoods, necessary for the settlement of the new ruling class, led to the recovery of a considerable quantity of archaeological material. Rodolfo Lanciani organized this material according to scientific criteria. In fact, in 1903, the talented archaeologist was in charge of the preparation of an area of the Palazzo dei Conservatori (which became a museum after it lost its function as the official site of the civic magistracy). He arranged the works of art according to the contexts of their place of origin with a criterion that, for the first time, favored the excavation data.

In the years of the "Governorship" (between 1925 and 1930), the structures of the Palazzo Caffarelli (which until the fifteenth century constituted with Palazzo Clementino a unique property adjacent to the Palazzo dei Conservatori) also became an integral part of the Capitoline Museums. A series of works of art that, until then, had been kept in the warehouses were finally displayed to the public in the Palazzo Caffarelli. This time, the arrangement of the Mussolini Museum, which subsequently took the name of the *Museo Nuovo* (New Museum), did not follow Lanciani's intended topographical organization. Instead, it followed an expository criterion intended to review the most significant phases of Greek art through Roman copies inspired by Greek originals. In the same years, the renovated *Antiquarium* was built on the Caelian Hill. It contained the material evidence of the most ancient history of the city, from the origins to the Republican period, and the daily objects used during the imperial age. Only in 1956 the creation of a new area of the Palazzo dei Conservatori, the *Braccio Nuovo* (the New Wing), permitted the enlargement of the museum. The Braccio Nuovo housed materials of noteworthy artistic and scientific relevance found as early as the Thirties during several urbanistic interventions. These archeological findings include sculptures belonging to the Republican or Proto-Imperial monuments, found on the slopes of the Campidoglio during the isolation of the hill, or originating from the excavations of Largo Argentina. In the same period, the subterranean gallery that connected different areas of the museum housed the Raccolta Epigrafica (Epigraphic Collection), currently under restoration.

The Future of the Museums

In the last decades, the continuation of the historic-artistic studies, of the archival research and, especially, of the investigations in the museums and warehouses, as well as the reassembling of sculptural groups and archaeological contexts created the need for a better arrangement of the achieved results. The restoration works of the Capitoline Museums led, in a first phase, to the creation of an original and decentralized expository site, the *Centrale Montemartini* (the Montemartini Power Plant). Simultaneously, the Capitoline Museums witnessed the renewal of new spaces, which will permit the public once again to enjoy all of those treasures which are, unfortunately, not yet exhibited. Currently, the Palazzo Caffarelli rooms house interesting temporary exhibits. In the future, the *Giardino Romano* (the Roman Garden) will witness the creation of new expository areas created with the purpose to display the equestrian group of Marcus Aurelius. Furthermore, the "Grande Campidoglio" (Great Campidoglio) project will enhance the landscape of the famous hill.

Frieze of the internal decoration of the Temple of Apollo Sosianus. In the background, the panorama of the industrial archaeology from the Ostiense area

Palazzo Nuovo

 Palazzo Senatorio
Tabularium

 Palazzo dei Conservatori
Clementino Caffarelli

VISITING THE MUSEUMS

The collections are so rich, and constitute so many
works of art dating to different periods and originating
from various places, that it has been necessary to choose
the most significant art pieces from the historic
and artistic point of view.
Nonetheless, we are convinced that the visitor,
enchanted by the beauty of the places, will come back
to discover the hidden curiosities.
The route begins at the Palazzo Nuovo, the premises
of the Capitoline Museum, located on the left
of the square for the visitor who goes up the staircase
of the hill.

PALAZZO NUOVO
CAPITOLINE MUSEUM

Capitoline Venus

**Ground Floor
Palazzo Nuovo**

 Ticket Office

Capitoline
Bookstore

Checkroom

I. II. III. Little Rooms on the
Ground Floor on the Right
Hand Side

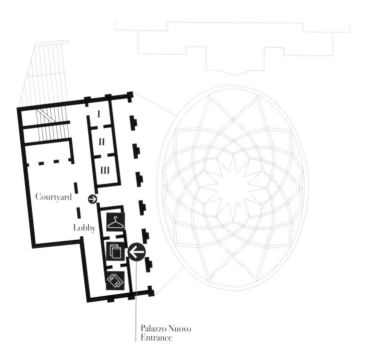

First Floor
Palazzo Nuovo

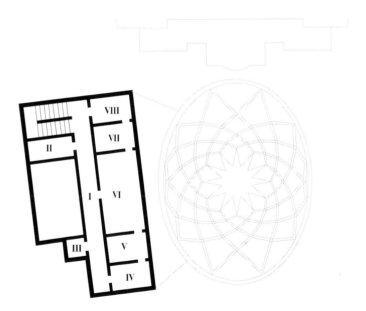

Atrium and Courtyard

The arrangement of the internal spaces of the ground floor recalls the environments of the Roman house (*domus*), which the patrician houses of the 18th century imitated. Symmetrical openings framed by travertine architraves and columns with wall partitions painted with plaster divide the internal colonnade. The exterior of the Palazzo Nuovo, decorated with niches with and without gables, is similarly divided. These openings house the largest statues and some masterpieces that once belonged to the Belvedere Collection in the Vatican and which afterwards were donated to the city of Rome. Roman inscriptions, mostly funerary, are located on the walls.

Beginning the visit from the right-hand side, the visitor comes across the colossal statue of *Minerva*. Probably, its model derives from one of the precious statues of Athena, which Pheidias made in Greece in the 5th century BC with the chryselephantine (i.e., with gold and ivory) or acrolithic (flesh in marble, garments in cloth or bronze) technique. The eye cavities were originally filled with hard stones and metal. The visible holes on the belt located on the waist and the still present studs on the chest were used in order to clamp on parts of different material. The cult image has been attributed to Pasiteles' circle—a sculptor from Magna Graecia who worked in Rome during the first century BC and who advocated the recovery of the technical and stylistic traditions of the past. Perhaps, the statue once decorated the temple of the goddess near the *Iseum Campensis* located in

Statue of Minerva

On the preceeding pages
Fountain of the
Courtyard with the
Marforio statue

Equestrian statue of the
emperor Marcus
Aurelius (A.D. 161-
180)

the proximity of the Church of Santa Maria sopra Minerva.

A skillfully constructed exedra conceals the retaining wall of the medieval structures of the Aracoeli and encloses the courtyard. The so-called Marforio fountain derives its name from the *Martis Forum* (Forum of Mars), i.e., the Forum of Augustus with the Temple of Mars *Ultor*, where it is thought that the statue originated. The figure of the river-god, originally part of the decoration of a fountain that

might date to the Flavian age (first century AD) was restored with the typical attributes of Ocean. This statue was very famous because when it was still located at the foot of the Campidoglio the Romans posted on it defamatory remarks against the government signed with the name of Pasquino. A commemorative inscription placed above the fountain records the year of the creation of the Capitoline Museum (1734). Beside the inscription is the bust of the pope who promoted the museum.

Two mirror image statues known as the *Satyrs "della Valle"* (named after the building that originally housed them) are located in niches on either sides of the Marforio. The two statues represent valuable pieces made in the late Hellenistic age depicting Pan, the Greek god of the countryside and nature. They were utilized in the theater of Pompey as telamons, i.e., figures of architectural support.

The courtyard still houses three granite columns decorated with a procession of priests with shaven heads who carry the attributes of the mystery cult of Isis. The three columns may date back to the emperor Domitian's renovation of the temple of the goddess in the Campus Martius. They were part of a small Egyptian collection (now located in the Palazzo dei Conservatori) that was originally placed in the side room where currently, for preservation reasons, the original *equestrian statue of Marcus Aurelius* has been temporarily sheltered after a complete restoration. The philosopher-emperor (161-180 AD), depicted in his mature years, makes a pacificatory gesture that epitomizes the wars he conducted to defend the boundaries of the Empire. But it is his Stoical philosophy that illuminates this charismatic figure with an austere serenity. The bronze group, originally belonging to a triumphal and gilded ancient monument, is made up of several parts fused together. It escaped the melting down of the bronze statues that took place in the Middle Ages because it was thought to represent "benedictory" Constantine, the symbol of Christianity. The eternally admired equestrian statue has always inspired several artists of different periods, starting with Donatello. It used to be located at the Lateran, then in the Campidoglio.

Continuing the visit of the atrium toward the right hand side, the visitors encounter the *colossal statue of Mars*, found near by the Forum of Nerva, serving as a perspective center for the monumental staircase. Probably, it is a copy made in the Flavian age (1st century AD) of the cult statue of the god in the temple of Mars Ultor in the Forum of Augustus. It had been placed outside in substitution of the original statue damaged by a fire. The helmet and armor decorated with imaginary animals, rich in symbolic significance, are particularly striking.

Little Rooms on the Ground Floor on the Right Hand Side

The three small spaces on the right hand side, overlooking the square deserve a stop before the visitor goes up to the main, upper, "noble" floor. They house epigraphic monuments of noteworthy interest.

Numerous private Roman portraits are located in the first room. On the left, the *funerary relief* stands out. Placed inside a niche with a flat frame, it depicts two living personages next to the deceased person, probably a freedman (freed slave) who lived in the first century BC. The fragments of Roman calendars that record the date of the new year (Caesar had determined that a year consisted of 365 days) are immured at the entrance. The second room houses the *large funerary altar of Titus Statilius Aper* (aper means wild boar). The altar is decorated on three of its sides. Instead, on the backside there is a cavity used to contain the ashes of the deceased. Under the figure of the deceased, an inscription reports that he was the master builder of a construction firm. Indeed, the work tools of this profession were sculpted on the sides. The monument is dated to the first century AD, when cremation was in vogue.

Funerary relief

In the third room a married couple is depicted lying on the colossal "*Alexander Severus*" *sarcophagus*. The features of their faces indicate that the piece dates to the 2nd century AD. All the sides of the Attic sarcophagus are decorated with high reliefs of scenes from Achilles' life.

Gallery

After ascending the two flights of the monumental staircase, the visitor arrives in the luminous gallery that connects the various rooms of the Museum. The *colossal statue of Hercules* is immediately visible. Beginning with its discovery, during the renewal of the church of Sant'Agnese fuori le Mura, the statue was endowed with luck. In fact, in the sixteenth century the piece underwent the sculptor Alessandro Algardi's complete restoration that slightly changed the statue's composition. Indeed,

On the following pages
Attic sarcophagus with scenes from Achilles' life

Colossal statue of
Hercules

Statue of a wounded
warrior

the artist transformed the *Hercules who domesticates the doe* into the *Hercules who kills the hydra*. The work of art is a Roman revision of a creation that can be ascribed to Lysippus (4th century BC) who, according to the sources, was the creator of a series of sculptures depicting the labors of Hercules.

The god Eros who strings a bow is a very high quality copy dating to the early imperial age of the original statue created by the same Greek master as well. With an elastic pose, almost out of balance, the young winged god extends his arms to string the bow with which he shot his arrows of love.

In the 18th century, an ancient bust, which was a re-elaboration of a statue of the *Discobolos* made by Myron (about 460 BC), was restored as a *statue of a wounded warrior*. Myron was an artist who made bronze statues and continuously experimented to best depict the body in motion in a three-dimensional space.

On the right side, the statue of *Leda with the swan* is a product of the circle of Timotheos (a Greek artist of the 4th century BC) The statue group, which was replicated in various copies from the 1st century BC, represents the erotic seduction theme of Zeus disguised as a swan to win over the mythical queen of Sparta.

The Capitoline Museum is extraordinarily rich with reproductions of typical subjects of the Hellenistic age. The interest in the aspects

Eros who strings the
bow

of daily life, studied in all of its forms, develops in this age, which conventionally begins with Alexander the Great's death (323 BC). So the *statue of the old drunken woman* belongs to a group of representations of genre figures which analyse with virtuoso fidelity the effects of physical decay, with an emphasis on the 'anthropological' study of the humblest strata of society. The Roman copy, reassembled from several fragments, is faithful to the character of the original in the delicacy of the drapery, in the realistic rendering of the veins and wrinkles of the skin, and the gaunt body of the woman shown hugging a bottle of wine in delirious ecstasy.

The representation of children, often depicted while playing, is also characteristic of the Hellenistic age. On the left-hand side, the small statue of the *baby Heracles who chokes the snakes* is a typical example of such a representation. Heracles' figure may represent the portrait of the Caracalla or Annius Verus, Marcus Aurelius' son. The expository route proceeds to two works on display in the Hall of the Faun. They are *the young boy choking the goose*, replica of a statue created by Boetius (2nd century BC), and *the young boy playing with a mask*.

Statue of old drunken woman

Hall of the Doves

The original *statue of the young girl with the dove*, located in the center of the room, belongs to the same cultural context. The reliefs of Greek funerary stelai made in the 5th and 4th centuries might have inspired the figurative motif of the statue. This hall derives its name from the famous mosaic found in the eighteenth century inside Hadrian's Villa in Tivoli. At that time, the name of the room was "The Miscellaneous Room" because it housed pieces (most of which belonged to the Albani Collection) of great typological variety. In modern times, the arrangement of the works of art only underwent minor changes: the portraits are still placed on shelves located along the walls decorated with sepulchral inscriptions. The frontal piece of a *sarcophagus depicting the Indian triumph of Bacchus*, dating to the period of Commodus (2nd century AD), has been immured at the entrance. The god leads a chariot drawn by panthers and is preceded by elephants and satyrs. Under the windows overlooking the courtyard, ancient glass display cases contain important bronze documents of the history of Rome and the *Tabula Iliaca*, a fragment of miniaturist low relief (1st century BC) depicted with scenes of the Homeric *Iliad* completed with inscriptions.

The *Mosaic of the Doves* was a figurative panel (*emblema*) located at the center of a mosaic floor depicted with simplified motifs. An astragal decoration frames the panel representing four doves depicted resting on the edge of a bronze vase. One of the doves is drinking from the vase. Under the

Palazzo Nuovo—Capitoline Museum

handle, a figure in relief seems to sustain the dove. It is a Hadrianic copy of an original created by Sosos, an artist who worked in Pergamon in the 2nd century BC. Paleochristian art transformed the dove into a symbol of the soul that draws from the fountain of salvation. The skillfully composed minute polychromatic tesserae (of marble and glass) create an astonishing pictorial effect.

The rendering of the *Mosaic of theatrical masks*, which in the 2nd century AD decorated an imperial building on the Aventine, is less accurate but still striking. The two "types" of the New Comedy—the young woman sad for the disasters that happened to her and the pensive and scornful slave—seem alive thanks to the skill of a mosaicist who gave much attention to the perspective values and play of light and shade.

The visitors who re-enter the **Gallery** and walk along it encounter two very well executed colossal heads of divinities located one in front of the other. These are the remaining fragments of cult statues created with the acrolithic technique. According to this technique, the flesh of the figures is made with marble and the rest of the body is made with wood structures covered in metallic sheets. The heads were carved out in the occipital region in order to lighten the weight of the statue. They may be examples of the artistic current that emerged in Rome in the second century BC in the work of Attic artists.

Colossal head
of goddess

On the following pages
Mosaic of the Doves
Mosaic of the theatrical
Masks

Cabinet of Venus

After walking along the Gallery, the visitor arrives at a small polygonal room on the right-hand side built at the beginning of the 19th century to create a charming setting, typical of a nymphaeum, for the *Capitoline Venus*. The sculpture, among the most famous and reproduced pieces of the collection, is made of a prestigious marble (which probably originated from the Greek island of Paros containing marble with wonderful transparent properties when viewed with light held at an oblique angle.) The statue was found in a perfect state of preservation—a recent restoration exalts the softness of the flesh—because its owner, during a period of danger, hid it inside a wall. The goddess is represented naked while she steps out of her ritual bath, symbolized by the vase and the cloth depicted next to her. This iconography dates back to a Hellenistic variation of the *Pudica* (modest) *Aphrodite*, created by Praxiteles in the middle of the 4th century BC for the Knidian sanctuary. The Capitoline replica, from the Antonine age, may have been meant to adorn the garden of a refined architectural complex.

Hall of the Emperors

At the end of the gallery, the visitor enters a room on the left-hand side where sixty-seven busts depicting Roman emperors and personages of the imperial circle are placed on a double row of shelves. Some of the portraits depict persons of unknown identity. Indeed, many of these probably represent portraits of private people. However, in

Capitoline Venus

the modern period the collectors, wishing to complete the series, arbitrarily assigned them names of emperors. Historically, numerous falsifications took place because the iconography of "rare" emperors was attributed to anonymous portraits according to the images depicted on coins. In the case of the sculptures of the Capitoline collection, one of the largest of its kind in the world, all of the portraits are ancient, and only some of the busts are modern. The sculptures in the room chronologically follow the development of the Roman portraiture dating from the Augustan age to the late-antique period and represent a figurative summary of the history of Rome. The Roman portrait develops from the variegated Greek-Hellenistic matrix. Indeed, the portrait of Alexander the Great represents the beginning of the Roman portraiture. He enjoyed being "theatrically" depicted according to differential schemes (as a hero, victorious general, philosopher, and god). He was represented with great physiognomic realism when his achievements were celebrated and in a more idealized fashion when he wanted to convey the idea of transcendence and divine assimilation. These two models inspire the two portraits of Augustus located in the room. The *Octavian "Actium type"* is located on the left of the window overlooking the square, and the *Augustus "Ara Pacis type"* is placed on the same level. The first portrait refers to the period immediately after the battle (31 BC) when Caesar's young adoptive son defeated Anthony and became the ruler of Rome. His hair is depicted with thick, ruffled locks, and his neck is turned sideways. In addi-

tion, the artist sculpted the face making great use of chiaroscuro that defines and characterizes the emperor's features. The second portrait, instead, depicts a mature emperor, composed and aware of his authority. The emperor's realistic physiognomy is disguised in a balanced structure, of classical trend, which recalls his portrait on the reliefs of the Ara Pacis. In the same fashion, the portraits of the women belonging to the imperial family (beginning with the *portrait of Livia*, Augustus' wife) show very few characterizing features, except for some details and, especially, the hairstyle which alone often allows the identification of the personage. This is the case of the very beautiful *portrait of Agrippina the Elder* (in the right corner), unfortunate wife of Germanicus. The features of the *Flavian Lady*'s face are very sophisticated and her tall and uneven scaffolding of ringlets is noticeable. She is located in front of the closed window. The hairstyle with a "ring-shaped" bun was in vogue for the entire Antonine period. The polychromatic bust of the *Roman Lady*, dating to the Alexander Severan age, is unique because it is composed of several parts, e.g., the marble hair insertions. It seems that the hair was interchangeable. The series of the emperors shows the evolution of the hair and beard styles. At first men were clean-shaven. Later they grew beards, "in the Greek manner," in order to seem inspired and philosophically committed. The *seated statue of Helen* dominates the center of the room. She was the mother of the emperor Constantine and the advocate of Christianity. The body into which her restored portrait has been inserted is a faithful copy of a famous statue of Aphrodite created in the middle of the 5th century BC by the Pheidian circle.

Hall of the Philosophers

The next room displays busts of poets, philosophers, and orators of Greek antiquity. In the Roman age and later, in the Renaissance, their images decorated public and private libraries, houses, villas and parks of rich and sensitive connoisseurs of the arts and philosophy. Many of the portraits represented here are imaginary reconstructions of the depicted intellectuals created in order to exalt the moral and spiritual values of the personages. In contrast, the portraits made during the Hellenistic age more faithfully reproduce the different physiognomies of the people represented. The *herms of Homer* (located immediately on the left of the entrance, on the lower shelf) are numerous. The poet's legendary blindness underlined his keen knowledge of the soul and destiny of humanity. On the upper shelf, the visitors find the statue of the philosopher *Socrates*. It was created fifty years after his death according to a model created by Lysippus on the basis of Plato's description. The *portrait of the mathematician Pythagoras* wearing a flat turban (below on the left before exiting the room) is interesting. In a *two-faced herm*, easily recognizable because of its central position, the master *Epicurus*, with raised eyebrows, and the pupil *Metrodorus* will always be together.

The *portrait of Cicero*, one of the most authentic portraits dating in the late-Republican period (1st

century BC), stands out among the imperial busts because of its dimensions and quality of execution. This statue faithfully depicts the man who was the politician who saved the country, as well as the famous orator and writer. The fragment of the sarcophagus where the *transferal of the body of Meleager* is sculpted in relief is located on the wall above *Cicero's portrait*. The depiction of this fragment clearly inspired Raphael when he created the *Deposition* currently located in the Galleria Borghese.

Great Hall
The very luminous hall is the quintessential space of the complex due to its dimension and monumentality. It was planned and decorated in order to house the sculptures currently displayed in it according to a decorative arrangement rather than the typological one that characterizes the previous rooms. Giant pilasters organized in vertical sections and subdivided into niches and faux doorways divide the walls. The extraordinary Baroque coffered ceiling decorated with octagons, rectangles, and mixed figures adorned with richly carved ceiling rosettes was made in the seventeenth century. The coat of arms of Innocent X Pamphili, responsible for the completion of the building, is located at the center of the ceiling. The large portal (arch-shaped with two winged victories made in stucco) is striking. It was created in the first half of the eighteenth century and it connects the hall with the gallery.
Two matching *Centaurs* (mythological creatures

Bust of Cicero

On the preceeding pages
Great Hall of the
Capitoline Museum

half man and half horse) are located in the middle of the hall. They were found during the excavations that took place in Hadrian's Villa in Tivoli in the 18th century. Aristeas and Papias created the sculptures made of a rare and prestigious marble (bigio morato). The sculptors came from Aphrodisias, a city located in Asia Minor, which boasted a school of extremely skillful artists who copied numerous Greek works for rich Roman commissioners. The attempt to provide the details of the Hadrianic period copies (2nd century AD) with the characteristics of metalwork as well as the use of colored marble might indicate that the original statue was made in bronze during the Hellenistic period. This period favored representations rich in anecdotal and moralizing details. The young Centaur is represented happily in motion and showing his prey. Instead, the older Centaur is represented tired and suffering from the pangs of love. Indeed, originally, a cupid clasped the Centaur's arms behind his back. Next to the large central glass window, the statue of the *"Capitoline type"* Amazon stands out representing one of the mythic warrior women especially honored in Asia Minor. In fact, the sources narrate that in the second half of the 5th century BC the most important Greek artists (such as Pheidias and Polyclitus) competed to establish the official type of the Amazon to be dedicated in the sanctuary of Artemis in Ephesus. The Amazon was no longer depicted as a ferocious fighter, but wounded and veiled with melancholy. This copy might closely resemble Polyclitus' winning model because of its rhythmic coherence.

"Furietti" Centaur

The statue by Sosikles, a Neo-Attic sculptor, was heavily restored in the 18th century.

Hall of the Faun

The itinerary ends with the last two rooms organized according to aesthetic principles that assign to the central sculptures the role of "masterpiece." Benedict fourteenth bought for the museum the prestigious rosso antico marble statue originating from Hadrian's Villa. Even though the delicate eighteenth century restoration involved numerous additions, the ancient image did not change considerably. The depiction is referable to a very diffuse typology in the Hellenistic environment where the taste for Dionysiac themes with bucolic and rural connotations developed. *The Faun*, half man and half animal, with the skin of a deer knotted on a shoulder, looks as if he is about to dance. This representation seems very suitable for Roman gardens (*horti*).

Again, the very careful rendering of the statue's anatomical details (i.e., the tense and raised muscles) and the drunken face's eye cavities (where vivid eyes made with hard stones and metallic eyelashes were placed) suggest that this copy originates from an original piece made in bronze. Like the *Centaurs* in the large hall, the School of Aphrodisias also made this statue. Among the inscriptions located in the wall on the right, the bronze table of the *Lex de imperio Vespasiani* stands out. The decree conferred special powers to the emperor in the 1st century AD Cola di Rienzo inflamed the Roman people's memory of the past greatness

Drunken Faun in rosso
antico marble

when he read and commented on those words (which were not engraved but cast).

Hall of the Faun

Hall of the Gladiator

This hall derives its name from the sculpture placed in its center, the *Capitoline Gaul*. In fact, when the statue became part of the Ludovisi Collection in 1734, the Gaul was erroneously thought to be a gladiator falling on his own shield. This work of art might be the most famous piece of the collections. Indeed, it was replicated on engravings and drawings numerous times. The statue represents a victim of the war that the Attalid kings of Pergamon waged against the Galatians in the 3rd century BC. The Greeks used to call "Galatians" the Celtic tribes (the Gauls of the Romans) that settled in a central region of modern Turkey. The warrior is depicted with his characteristic attributes (shield, torque on his neck, heroic nudity, mustache and hair locks besmeared with chalk to scare the enemy). His wound is a very visible sign of his final moment of resistance to his pain. The *dying Gaul*, as well as the group of the *Gaul committing suicide* originating from the same Ludovisi Collection (currently located at Palazzo Altemps), almost surely derive from a bronze monument that Attalus I (241-197 BC) created in Pergamon to celebrate the victories over the Galatians. According to an acceptable historical reconstruction, the despot of an atelier from Pergamon might have commissioned these copies in order to commemorate in a private circle the conquest of Gaul (46–44 BC) The statues were made in Asiatic marble. They were found in the vil-

On the following pages
Capitoline Gaul

Amazon

la Ludovisi in Porta Pinciana (where in the past the *horti* of Caesar were located.)

Other replicas of noteworthy quality surround the *Gaul*. The *wounded Amazon* dates back to the model that Pheidias sculpted for the competition that took place in Ephesus. Indeed, the drapery shows a delicate and theatrical taste recalling the Amazons located in the decoration of the Parthenon.

The very beautiful statue of *Hermes* is traditionally identified with Antinous, the young man beloved of the Emperor Hadrian, from whose estates at Tivoli it comes. The *resting Satyr* is one of the most known replicas of the original created by Praxiteles, (4th century BC) The image of the young boy might have decorated little woods and nymphaea (fountains). His ears are pointy and emerge from thick, golden locks of hair. He is depicted in a moment of relaxation, softly leaning on a tree trunk. By the window, the charming Rococo group of *Eros and Psyche* symbolizes the tender union between the human soul and divine love. The statue group theme dates back to Platonic philosophy, which enjoyed success in the artistic world as early as the early Hellenistic period.

PALAZZO DEI CONSERVATORI

Courtyard of the Palazzo dei Conservatori
with fragments of the colossal statue
of Constantine

Ground Floor
Palazzo dei Conservatori

 Ticket Office

 Capitoline Bookstore

 Checkroom

 Handicapped-accessible
elevator

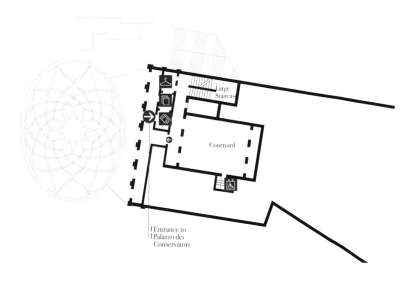

Large
Staircase

Courtyard

Entrance to
Palazzo dei
Conservatori

**First Floor
Palazzo dei Conservatori**

 Capitoline
Bookstore

 Handicapped-
accessible elevator

I. Hall of the Horatii and
Curiatii
II. Hall of the Captains
III. Hall of the Triumphs
IV. Hall of the She-wolf
V. Hall of the Geese
VI. Hall of the Eagles
VII. Green Hall
VIII. Yellow Hall
IX. Pink Hall
X. Hall of the Tapestries
XI. Hall of Hannibal
XII. The Chapel
XIII. XIV. XV. Halls of the Modern *Fasti*

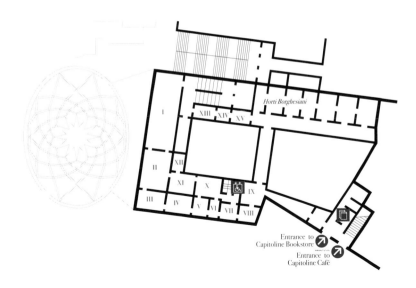

Courtyard

Since the very early creation of the collections, the courtyard has represented the best location for displaying the ancient works of art. The courtyards of the aristocratic buildings were used for the same function. Some traces of the original ogival arches used as the entrance to the display of the statues are still visible on the right side of the courtyard. The fragments of the colossal *acrolithic statue of Constantine* (313–324 AD) are placed next to the right wall. They were found in the 15th century in the western apse of the Basilica of Maxentius in the Roman Forum. The emperor himself was responsible for the completion of the Basilica. Only the exposed flesh of the statue, representing Constantine seated on his throne, was made of marble. They were mounted on a supporting structure (made of wood and masonry) covered in drapery made of gilded bronze or veneer of precious polychromatic marbles. In this representation, Constantine is depicted as a god. Even though the emperor's physiognomical features are compressed into abstract shapes, his traits are depicted with a strong realism (aquiline nose, jutting chin, long and thin lips). The enormous eyes, which in their fixed gaze seem to look beyond what is visible, are the most striking feature of the statue.

The reliefs from the Temple, which in 145 AD Antoninus Pius dedicated to his adoptive father Hadrian (deified after his death), are arranged on the left side of the courtyard. The extant remains of the Temple are located in Piazza di Pietra incorporated in the Palazzo della Borsa (the Stock

Exchange Building). The decorations of the reliefs include plinths with war trophies alternated with bases representing the personifications of the subdued *Provinces*, recognizable by their specific attributes.

The unique group of the *goddess Roma* was placed in the back of the courtyard located inside the portico added in the 18th century. Toward the middle of the 16th century, Cardinal Cesi composed this group with sculptural fragments dating to different periods and made of different styles in his garden in the Borgo. Currently, the statue is located between two *prisoner statues*, whose precious marble (*bigio morato*) makes them comparable to the series of prisoners in the Forum of Trajan, constructed after Trajan's victory over the Dacians. These works of art attest that in the 16th century artists favored audacious mixtures (as the Romans themselves in the antiquity) and restorations that often were assemblies and distortions that changed the original meaning of the work.

Monumental Staircase
(First and Second Landing)

The visitors ascend to the first landing of the monumental staircase from the lobby of the building where the original inscription (belonging to the previously mentioned donation of the Lateran bronzes by Sixtus IV) is displayed. In the 16th century, four *large historical reliefs of the imperial age* were immured in the first landing. The first three, part of a series of eleven panels (eight of which were reused for the decoration of the attic story of

Palazzo dei Conservatori

the Arch of Constantine) came from official monuments dedicated to Marcus Aurelius between 176 and 180 AD. Going up the stairs, the visitors find on the right hand side the panel depicting the emperor offering sacrifices in front of the Temple of Capitoline Jupiter, represented here in one of his most detailed representations. The following reliefs, instead, celebrate the emperor's triumph and clemency over the defeated enemy. He is depicted with a stance that recalls the emperor's pose on the bronze statue placed on the piazza. The fourth panel, originally belonging to a public monument built in honor of Hadrian, shows the emperor's entrance into the city.

One of the two panels that decorated the so-called Arch of Portugal on Via Lata (the current via del Corso) is mounted on a wall of the second landing, which has a vault enriched by spectacular stuccowork. The arch was a late antique monument, made with discarded material, which was later destroyed in the 17th century to enlarge the road. In this relief, the emperor Hadrian is in charge of the distribution of food to Roman children.

Apartment of the Conservators

The state apartments of the building, which housed the magistracy of the Conservators, are located on the first floor. The fresco cycles and sumptuous decoration—from the engraved and painted ceiling to the sculpted leaves, from the 18th century stuccowork to the eighteenth century tapestries—are the result of several interventions that took place over the course of several centuries. The constant

Relief of a monument built in honor of Marcus Aurelius: the emperor offers a sacrifice in front of the Capitoline Temple

choice of the same subjects, focused on the narration of the main episodes evocative of Rome during the monarchic and Republican periods, confers uniformity to the decorations of the rooms and attests to the continuation of their symbolic meaning of exalting civic virtues.

Hall of the Horatii and Curiatii

The large hall, used for important ceremonies, received its current dimensions after Michelangelo's restructuring of the palace, and was used for the sessions of the Public Council. Toward the end of the sixteenth century, Cavalier d'Arpino (a prominent personality of the Roman Mannerism) was entrusted with the task of depicting with striking images the legendary account of the origins of Rome according to Titus Livy. The painter conceived the frescoes as unfolded tapestries decorating the walls where vertical bands adorned with festoons of fruit and flowers, war trophies and lustral vases divide the episodes. A painted frieze made of faux marble and decorated with monochrome medallions depicting episodes from Roman history related with the theme represented above runs along the base of the fresco. Furthermore, a heavy red curtain supported by telamons is draped on the short sides and hangs over the depicted scenes. Cupids represented next to the telamons hold the insignia of the Roman people. In the first fresco located at the back of the room, Faustulus' *discovery of the She-Wolf* with the twins on the banks of the Tiber is depicted in a spacious and sunny landscape.

78   Palazzo dei Conservatori

The Battle of the Romans versus the People of Veii and Fidenae follows on the left wall. In this composition, the author expressed his ability to depict spatial organization and dramatic expression. The lying warrior represented in the foreground already echoes the Capitoline Gaul. Next to this scene, the Battle of the Horatii and Curiatii (1612-1613) gives its name to the hall. The battle was the decisive event in the conflict between Rome and Alba Longa for the supremacy of Latium. It seems that the painter sublimated the excellence of the Roman people while exalting the value of the single hero. The last frescoes were created more than twenty years later with his pupils' assistance. On the right wall, Romulus traces the furrow of the squared city, Numa Pompilius institutes the cult of the Vestals and, on the short adjacent side, the Rape of the Sabines takes place. It seems that these pieces lack freshness of style and originality even though they are depicted with a harmonious range of colors.

The sculptures of Urban VIII (made in marble between 1635 and 1640 by Gian Lorenzo Bernini and his school) and Innocent X (cast in bronze by Algardi between 1645 and 1650) are arranged facing each other, solemn and vivacious benedictory keepers of such a magnificent context.

The room will house the elements of the colossal bronze statue of Constantine until the restructuring of the museum is completed. In the Middle

Colossal bronze statue of Constantine

On the following pages Hall of the Horatii and Curiatii. Cavalier d'Arpino, *The Battle of the Horatii and Curiatii* (1612-1613)

Ages, they belonged to the Lateran treasure. As previously mentioned, they were placed in the Campidoglio in 1471 when Sixtus IV's donation took place. The head, impressive both for its colossal dimensions and for the intensity of its features, is similar to the portraits of Constantine created in the last period of his life. The statue is the result of the assembly of separate pieces that, possibly, were originally gilded. The hand in the act of holding the globe, symbol of the celestial dominance on earth belongs to the statue. The work, as well the acrolith in the courtyard, harmonized with the imposing architectural background characteristic of that period and with the late antique ideal that the emperors were in direct contact with the supernatural world.

In the Great Hall, the glare of the statue of *Hercules made in gilded bronze*, catches the visitors' eye. The statue was found during the pontificate of Sixtus IV in the area of the Forum Boarium adjacent to the medieval church of Santa Maria in Cosmedin. A chronology that spans as late as to the 2nd century AD. has been proposed for this statue, which underwent some restoration. However, according to a convincing theory, the piece belonged to a cult statue located in a round temple dedicated to the Greek hero by Scipio Æmilianus in the 2nd century BC. The figure is depicted holding the apples of the Hesperides in his hand with the intent of alluding to the Hispanic enterprises of his family. The proportions and the decisive rendering of the body indicate that Greek prototypes dating to the 4th century BC, close to the Lysippic style, inspired the

Statue of Hercules
made in gilded bronze

statue. A recent hypothesis suggests a direct derivation of the statue from a bronze mold dating to that period.

Hall of the Captains
The visitors enter the room previously called Room of the Audiences through two doors with leaves richly decorated with reliefs. Currently the space is called the Room of the Captains because it houses numerous commemorative inscriptions and some honorary statues and Baroque busts depicting generals of the Church army who distinguished themselves in war. *Marcantonio Colonna*, captain of the pontifical fleet who, in 1571, fought at Lepanto against the Turks and *Carlo Barberini*, pope Urban VIII's brother, are the most noteworthy commanders present in the room. Carlo Barberini's statue was created by the artist Algardi's restoration of a reused Roman cuirass sculpture (he added the legs, arms, and shield) and by Bernini's forceful marble portrait.
The large frescoes decorating the room, made by Tommaso Laureti (Sebastiano del Piombo's pupil) in the last decades of the 16th century, are especially interesting. The figurative style of the late Roman Mannerism influenced the artist's style which shows frequent references to Michelangelo and Raphael's works of art. The celebration of the ancient Romans' virtues and courage is depicted with lively color and monumentality through examples taken from the history of the first Republican period. The painted scene with the *Justice of Brutus*, who does not hesitate to sentence

his own children to death, was purposefully placed in the back wall where the Conservators were seated in the tribunal. Instead, the *Victory at Lake Regillus* against the Tuscolani is celebrated on the left wall. The right wall depicts *Horatius Cocles* defending the Pons Sublicius (Sublicius Bridge) during the siege of the Etruscan king Porsenna, represented on the entrance wall in front of *Mucius Scaevola*.

Tommaso Laureti,
Justice of *Brutus*
(1587-1594)

Hall of the Triumphs

This room still retains one of the oldest wooden ceilings of the building (1568). The recent restoration enhanced the liveliness of the colors and the importance of the prestigious carvings with war trophies. A frescoed frieze made by the pupils of Daniele da Volterra runs under the ceiling. The room takes its name from the frieze because it celebrates the consul Æmilius Paulus' triumph over Perseus, king of Macedonia (167 BC). The painters faithfully narrated the development of the procession according to the description of the ancient historian Plutarch. However, the artists formally followed the classical historical relief models. The painting depicts the ritual ascension of the victor to the Campidoglio. However, the façade of the Palazzo dei Conservatori interestingly substitutes the Temple of Capitoline Jupiter in a play of cross-references between present and past. Giacomo Della Porta renewed the façade by adding the large window and terrace in the center. The paintings of del Piazza (*Deposition*, on slate, 1614) and of G. Francesco Romanelli (*Saint Francesca Romana*, 1638) were purposefully created for installation in this room. Both paintings are filled with an evocative luminarism. In the middle of the fifteenth century, Pietro da Cortona created in his youth the large canvas depicting the *Victory of Alexander against Darius* in order to celebrate Alessandro Sacchetti, commander of the pontifical troops and commissioner of many of the artist's works of art housed in the Capitoline picture gallery.

The room houses three historical bronze statues. *The Spinario* is located in the center of the room. The piece is a small sculture depicting a young boy pulling out a thorn from his foot. In the Renaissance, the piece was one of the most studied and imitated ancient works of art due to the unique

The Spinario

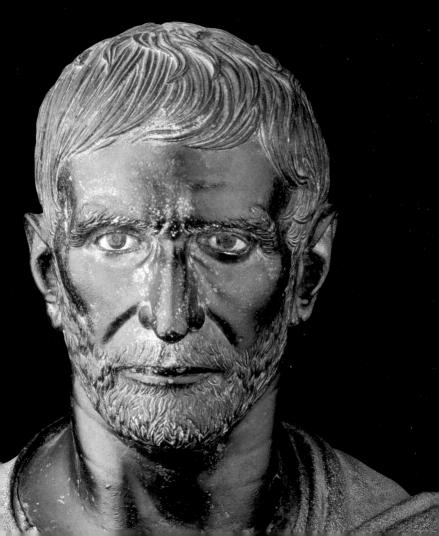

and graceful pose of the figure, caught in an unusual gesture. The statue is an eclectic creation made in the 1st century BC. Indeed, it is comprised of different formal models. For example, the artist placed the Severe style head derived from Greek works of art dating to the middle of the 5th century BC on a tender body of Hellenistic derivation (third–2nd century BC).

The statue of the *Camillus* made with silver eyes, instead, dates back to the classicism of the 1st century AD. The statue was interpreted for a long time as a "Gypsy" due to its soft and elegant hairstyle, the feminine features of the face, and the soft drapery of the garment. The young boy assigned to the cult (*camillus*) originally held on his right hand a small cup for the ritual libation.

The magnificent portrait of the so-called *Brutus Capitolinus* (the bust is modern) is striking for its extraordinary expressive power reached through the physiognomic study of the personage and a refined technique of production (the eyes made of ivory and glassy paste are ancient). The antiquarian culture of the fifteenth century identified the portrait with Junius Brutus, the first Roman consul. However, the identification and understanding of the work of art raise many problems. Indeed, the Roman culture of the Republican age influenced the iconography of the piece attributable in some aspects to the Greek portrait models of poets and philosophers. Currently,

very few bronze portraits belonging to the
Republican period, between the 4th and 3rd centu-
ry BC (the head is similar to the painted portrait of
Velthur Velcha in the Tomb of the Shields in
Tarquinia), remain.

Hall of the She-Wolf

Originally, this room was a loggia with three arches facing the city (the traces of the loggia are still
visible on the external wall). *The She-Wolf* was
moved from the fifteenth century façade of the
building to this room in the middle of the sixteenth
century on the occasion of Michelangelo's architectural interventions. The artist's plan also contem-
plated the arrangement of the *Consular and
Triumphal Fasti* fragments (found in the Roman
Forum) on the back wall of the courtyard. In this
space, the fragments were recomposed closely to
their original arrangement. As a result, the valuable
cycle of frescoes created by the Bolognese painter
Iacopo Ripanda under the pontificate of Julius II
(1503–1513) were damaged. Currently, the scenes
are difficult to interpret (even though Æmilius
Paulus' triumph has been securely identified) also
because they were further damaged by the inser-
tion of two commemorative inscriptions that left
only four parts untouched.

The *Consular and Triumphal Fasti* are an important
aid for the reconstruction of Roman history. The
inscriptions report the lists of the magistrates present during the foundation of the Republic and of
those who also celebrated the triumph beginning
with Romulus. The list ends in the Augustan age. In

91

Capitoline She-wolf

fact, these inscriptions were placed on the internal walls of an arch dedicated to Augustus in 19 BC in memory of his victorious campaign against the Parthians.

We have already discussed the importance of the *She-Wolf* for the history of the city and of the collections. However, research (reviewed in a recent exhibition) proved the autonomy of the creation of the wolf that, as it appears from the almost heraldic and individual pose, had nothing to do with the twins and the legend of the origins of Rome. Very skillful Etruscan workers produced the bronze—the earth used in casting found inside came from the valley of the Tiber located between Orvieto and Rome, the lead of the alloy came from Sardinian mines—and carefully studied the contemporaneous works of art originating from Magna Graecia. On stylistic bases, the statue dates to the end of the first quarter of the 5th century BC. In this period, the figurative naturalism (observe the wolf's muzzle almost modeled from life), not yet influenced by the anatomical perfectionism that preceded the classic idealism, reflects the decorative stylization (see the hair tufts on the main and along the back) of the formal late archaic conception.

Hall of the Geese

The room regained the pleasant decorative unity desired by Paul III Farnese (1534–1549) whose emblems of the lily and lightning are depicted on the wall containing the window. The frieze is of great interest; its elegant motifs frame scenes of ancient games depicted on the background of imaginary or real landscapes, such as the view of the Piazza del Campidoglio with the Church of Santa Maria in Aracœli before the Farnese interventions. The room derives its name from two small *bronze geese* made in the Roman age, traditionally interpreted as legendary Capitoline geese that saved Rome from the Gallic invasion by raising the alarm. This space also houses an 18th century *portrait of Michelangelo* made in bronze and placed on a bust of marble. The portrait is derived from Daniele da Volterra's portrait, which was based on the death mask of the artist. The beautiful head of *Medusa* which Bernini sculpted in 1630 is striking. Her double nature, human and monstrous, is accentuated by the different surface finish of the marble, rough snake-like hair and a polished-smooth face.

Gian Lorenzo Bernini (1598-1680), *Medusa*

Hall of the Eagles

The refined decoration of this small environment is contemporary with the decoration of the previous room. Interesting views of ancient Rome, such as the view of the Capitoline square where the equestrian statue of Marcus Aurelius had been recently moved and the restructuring of the palaces had just begun, are depicted in the frieze of this room framed by grotesques. The room was the wardrobe of the Conservators and it derives its name from the two imperial sculptures placed on the sides of

On the following pages
Gian Lorenzo Bernini,
Medusa, detail

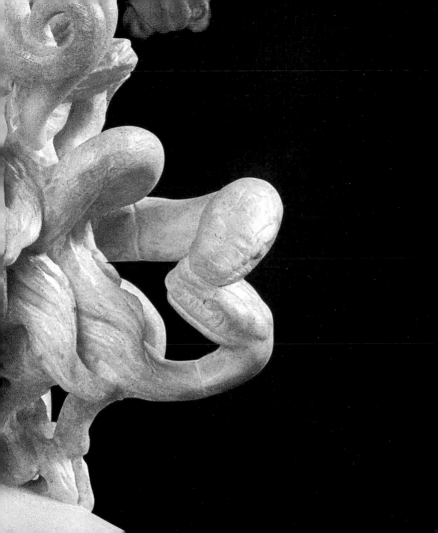

the door on columns made of cipollino marble. The small format copy of the unique Hellenistic *cult statue* of the Temple of Artemis in Ephesus is noteworthy. Its limbs are made in bronze and the body in marble. Bull testicles, symbol of fecundity, and figures of animals and bees hang from the body because the goddess also was their patron.

A series of Roman emperors' busts is displayed along the walls of the **Green Room.**
The precious table with a cult function (4th century AD) is placed at the center of the **Yellow Room**, where there are two glass display cases containing a rich collection of ancient marbles. The edge of the table is decorated with *scenes taken from Achilles' life*. The original element was reused in the decoration of the church of the Aracœli built in the 13th century by the Cosmati's studio, which also produced the prestigious inlay of colored marbles and glassy pastes. Hadrian's portrait made in a greenish alabaster stands out in a corner of the room. The 18th century restoration provided the statue with a disturbing gaze. The use of rare Egyptian material and the sophisticated modeling indicate that this work of art is one of the very high quality products of the workshops of the court.
In the **Pink Room**, two young girls, one on the other's shoulders, play the *ephedrismós*, a very popular group pastime in the classic Greece. In late classical times the singular position of the figures prompted a striving for complex grouping, the study of drapery and the rendering of movement. The discovery of a similar group in the city of Tegea

98   Palazzo dei Conservatori

made it possible to recognise the sculpture—originally a temple ornament—as the fruit of a passion for collecting among wealthy Romans which led to numerous masterpieces of Greek art being brought to Italy.

Hall of the Tapestries

The visitors who walk back through these small environments arrive into a room that houses some of the most ancient decorations of the palace: the magnificent coffered wooden ceiling and the frescoes (1544) made by Daniele da Volterra's circle. In these frescoes, the depiction of famous ancient sculptures, such as the *Hercules*, *Laocöon*, and *Apollo Belvedere* (found in that period) alternate with the representation of salient episodes from Scipio Africanus' life and the narration of Jupiter's mythical loves. In the 18th century, the room was entirely renewed in order to house the *baldacchino* of the papal throne. Thus, precious tapestries made in the Roman factory of San Michele covered the walls of the room. They depicted the works of art kept in the Campidoglio, such as Rubens' canvas with Romulus and Remus nursed by the *She-Wolf* and *Roma Cesi*, at the foot of which the artist Corvi placed the personifications of the rivers Tiber and Anio in his preparatory drawings.

Currently, the latter tapestry provides the backdrop for the *group of Commodus depicted as Hercules and flanked by two Tritons*. This piece was found on the Esquiline Hill, in a subterranean room of the *Horti Lamiani* complex. It is extraordinarily well preserved because it probably had

Hall of the Tapestries, wooden ceiling (1544)

Group of Commodus depicted as Hercules flanked by two Tritons

been kept hidden in antiquity. Two *sea-Tritons*, part of a larger sculptural composition, signify the apotheosis of the emperor-god depicted as Hercules. In memory of some of Hercules' labors, the emperor assimilated the Greek hero's attribut-

es: the lion skin, club, and the apples of the Hesperides. The bust is placed on a base decorated with symbolic allegories indicating the commemorative intent of the group.

Hall of Hannibal

The next room preserves the most ancient ceiling of the palace and, at the same time, contains the original decoration of the fresco attributed to Iacopo Ripanda's workshop (1508–1513). The cycle, rich in antiquarian references that witness the Bolognese school's interest toward classical antiquity, narrates episodes taken from the Punic wars. The scene with *Hannibal in Italy* is familiar, depicting the Carthaginian general wearing a naively-depicted oriental looking turban and riding his legendary elephant.

The magnificent *Crater of Mithridates Eupator*, king of Pontus (120–63 BC) is displayed in this room. It was found in Antium in Nero's Villa and it might have arrived in Italy as Sulla or Pompey's spoil of war. Indeed, the vase recalls the sumptuous triumphal processions that took place at the end of the conquest campaigns in the East when the most precious works of art taken away from the enemy and displayed in public.

The Chapel

Recent restorations contributed to the reopening of the ancient chapel of the palace dedicated to Mary and the Saints Peter and Paul, protectors of the city who are depicted on the altarpiece. The grand stucco decorations and the antependium decorated with precious marble inlays depicting bees, the symbol of Urban VIII Barberini (1623–1644), were restored as well. The detached fresco depicting the *Virgin and Child with Angels*, made at the end of the 15th century, hides the grating that allowed the Conservators and their retinue to attend the sacred functions from the room of the Captains.

Iacopo Ripanda's workshop, *Hannibal in Italy* (circa 1508-1509)

Halls of the Modern *Fasti*

Statue of Marsyas

The inscriptions, recording the names of the civic magistrates chronologically in their leadership of Rome, beginning in 1640, are displayed along the walls.

In the second room, the magnificent statue of *Marsyas*, is a jewel of the collection. It is a copy made in the Augustan age from a Hellenistic original, found in the horti of Maecenas. The work of art depicts the silenus who dared to challenge Apollo in a musical competition after he obtained Athena's flute. The Muses were the judges of the contest. The god managed to win with a stratagem, but he inflicted a cruel torture on the daring antagonist by skinning him alive. Purple *pavonazzetto* marble was specifically used in order to reproduce effect of flayed flesh. The figure hung on a pine tree, with tense muscles and a suffering face, is a true masterpiece of expressionistic art, the inspiration of many crucifixions.

Egyptian Collection

A little bit further, the small Egyptian collection resides temporarily. Mainly, it includes materials originating from the Temple of Isis and Serapis in the Campus Martius whose granite columns remained in the courtyard of the Palazzo Nuovo. The visitors can admire a white marble capital belonging to the columns with decorations imitating palm branches, a pink granite crocodile, a black granite sparrowhawk, and two gray granite baboons dating back to the last independent period of Egypt before Alexander the Great. A basanite sphinx of the

Relief from the Arco
di Portogallo: Hadrian
assists in the apotheosis
of Sabina

Pharaoh Amasis II (568-526 BC) whose head was
deliberately damaged due to *damnatio memoriæ*, is
displayed among the other works of art.

Monumental Staircase
(Second and Third Landings)
The visitors who go back toward the monumental
staircase find, embedded in a niche on the second

landing, the statue of *Carlo d'Angiò* on a throne. He was a senator of Rome during the end of the 13th century. The work of art is unanimously attributed to the Roman activity of Arnolfo di Cambio on the basis of stylistic and historical data (the artist worked for the king of Sicily), although the sources have never documented the work of art.

The visitors, who arrive at the third landing of the monumental staircase that leads to the Picture Gallery, find the second Hadrianic historical relief belonging to the Arch of Portugal on the left wall. The relief depicts the *Apotheosis of Sabina* who, on a female winged figure (*Æternitas*), ascends into Heaven from the flames that burned her body. The emperor Hadrian participates in the divinization of his wife (whom he did not love) in the company of the young personification of the Campus Martius, where the event took place. The bright panels made in *opus sectile* depicting tigers attacking calves are immured facing each other. These are two of the few remaining fragments (another two unique fragments are kept in Palazzo Massimo alle Terme) belonging to the magnificent pagan decoration made with polychromatic marble intarsio from the so-called Basilica of Junius Bassus. This consul promoted the construction of the basilica near Santa Maria Maggiore between 325 and 350 AD.

On the following pages Panel in opus sectile *with polycromatic marbles from the Basilica of Junius Bassus, representing a tiger attacking a calf*

**Second Floor
Picture Gallery**

 Capitoline Café

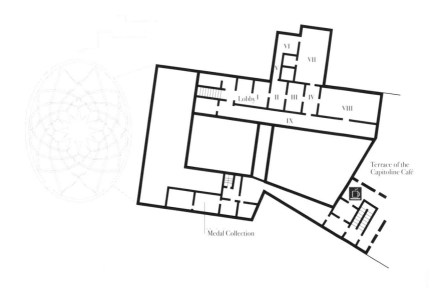

CAPITOLINE PICTURE GALLERY

In the rooms that Ferdinando Fuga purposefully built above the Capitoline archives Benedict XIV instituted, in 1749, the first public gallery in Rome following the purchase of the painting collections belonging to the marquis Sacchetti and the prince Pius of Savoia. The dispersion of these works of art into the antiquarian market was avoided with the intention of facilitating the study of the stylistic and iconographic evolution of the past artistic production for the young artists enrolled in the Accademia del Nudo (Academy of the Nude), originally located in the Campidoglio. Throughout the centuries, the collection witnessed many variations, such as the number of works displayed in it and their arrangement. Even in the last decades further donations and purchases enriched the collection, although its expository display (arranged according to epochs and schools) did not substantially change. The recent restoration of the interior and numerous paintings, together with new information panels enhance visitors' enjoyment.

Hall I

The first room houses a group of tempera wooden panel paintings originating from central Italy and dating to a period spanning from the Middle Ages to the Renaissance. Religious subjects and different formats characterize the works of art. The visitor can admire fragments of polyptychs and large-dimension art works originally produced to decorate altars. The central panel of a polyptych might represent the *Trinity* of the Tuscan artist Niccolò di Pietro Gerini. The piece was produced in the first years of the 15th century and depicts the commissioner in a reduced scale as a sign of humility toward the divine.

Cola dell'Amatrice's painting of the Dominican *Death and Assumption of the Virgin Mary* belongs to the following century (1515–1516). The artist was very active in Ascoli Piceno, where the piece was created. The scene is divided stylistically into two registers: in the lower (more efficacious) one, a revision in the style of Luca Signorelli is evident.

In addition, the large wooden panel depicting the *Presentation at the Temple* is striking. The Bolognese artists Francia and Passerotti, who rendered the painting surfaces with a glazed smoothness, created the panel for a church located in their city.

Hall II

16th century Ferrara is represented in this room. Ferrara was the site of the refined Estense family's court, and a lively cultural center (think of Ariosto and Tasso) rich with successful artistic workshops. Garofalo owned the main workshop whose elegant

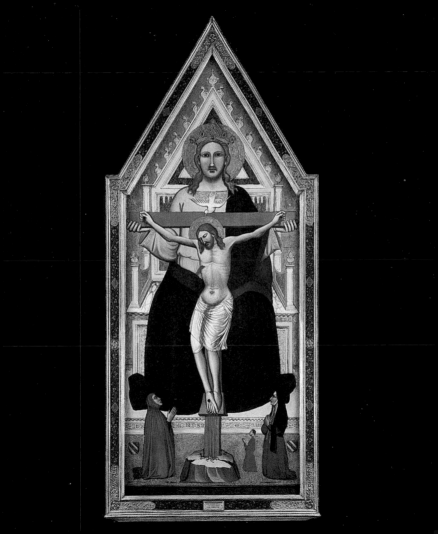

Dosso Dossi (Giovanni Luteri, ? circa 1489- Ferrara 1542), *Holy Family*

Tiziano (Titian) Vecellio (Pieve di Cadore circa 1490- Venice 1576), *Baptism of Christ*

Annunciation is admirable. In the Ferrarese painting, the bright Venetian spectrum of colors originally blended with a solid drawing structure and monumental framework of the figures, typical of Central Italy as the Dosso Dossi's *Holy Family* exemplifies. In the large altarpiece, painted in circa 1527, the artist concentrated on the affectionate relationship among Saint Joseph, the baby Jesus, and the Virgin whose serpentine pose recalls Raphael's *Sibyls* in Santa Maria della Pace in Rome.

Hall III

The revolution of color, a key feature of Venetian painting during the 16th century, is evident in the *Baptism of Christ*, one of the youthful masterpieces (created in about 1512) in which Titian favored light tones extended on the background. In addition, the portrait of the commissioner reveals the precocious maturity of the artist. The commissioner was a Spanish merchant who, dressed in dark colors, participated in an evangelic episode after his wife's death.

The Portrait of the Crossbowman that Lorenzo Lotto painted during his last refuge in the Marche (1551–1552) is noteworthy for its delicate naturalism and peculiar anti-rhetorical vein, not oblivious, however, of Titian's characteristic emphasis on tones of color.

114   Capitoline Picture Gallery

Giovanni Girolamo Savoldo (Brescia circa 1480 – Venice 1548), *Portrait of a woman*

The magnificent *Portrait of a woman* from Savoldo echoes the Lombard realism through the artist's virtuous workmanship of the garment details and the acute psychological research strengthened by the symbolism of the objects (for example, the small prayer book indicates the noblewoman's devotion).

Furthermore, by observing the *Rape of Europa* created by Veronese, it becomes clear why Venetian painting greatly influenced the European painting as late as the middle of the eighteenth century. In

Capitoline Picture Gallery

this canvas, the mythological episode (Zeus disguised as a white bull leads the young Europe to the island of Crete) enables the artist to implement his skill in depicting scenery through the successful use of vibrant colors in the splendid depiction of decorative details. This painting is a copy of the piece located in the Palazzo Ducale in Venice (1580).

Hall IV

This room allows a comparison with the adjacent rooms that house seventeenth century masterpieces created in Rome. The city was the meeting and formation place for artists with different origins. The painter Mola, from Ticino, was one of them and was the representative of the neo Venetian current. He painted *Diana and Endymion* in 1660. This painting is an example of the paintings "da camera" (of the room) characterized by biblical, knightly, or, as in this case, mythological subjects very much in demand during that period. A romantic atmosphere permeates this nocturnal scene where the Moon (Diana) contemplates the shepherd Endymion, who Zeus provided with an endless sleep in exchange for eternal youth.

Hall V

In this transition space, there is another example of this "minor" production. Around 1600, the Cavalier d'Arpino painted *Diana the Huntress* before he was put in charge of the decoration of the Room of the Horatii and Curiatii. Copies of famous works of art are placed along the walls. Most of them were from Emilia (see the *Virgin Mary of Albinea* inspired by a lost original made by Correggio) and were highly requested in the painting market.

Hall VI

This room is dedicated to the radical renewal introduced by the Bolognese painting with the foundation of the Accademia dei Carracci (Ludovico, Agostino, and Annibale) which influenced all Italian pictorial research. The minor works of art of these painters (Guido Reni, whose work represents the epitome of Baroque classicism, was one of their pupils) represent this new type of devotional art aware of the profound religious sensitivity in the spirit of the Counter Reformation. In the *Saint Sebastian* (circa 1615), Guido Reni favored the mysticism of the episode rather than the saint's suffering. The saint's body clearly recalls the classical sculpture that the artist studied when he was in Rome. The quality of the landscape, animated by small figures painted with the point of the paintbrush, and the chromatic play between the silvery white of the figure and the bluish greens of the background are striking. The numerous works of art of the last period displayed in this room represent the research of the ideal beauty that led to the creation of a painting free of any mimetic intent from the external reality. The pose and drapery of the *Girl With a Crown* were inspired by ancient sculpture. However, the fluid stroke and the absence of color almost render the figure a bodiless entity. In the *Blessed Soul*, found in the study of the artist upon his death (1642), the religiosity of Reni (beyond the classical references) is expressed in the

Guercino (Giovanni
Francesco Berbieri,
Cento 1591 – Bologna
1666), *Burial of Saint
Petronilla*

pure and abstract image of the soul that ascends to
the sky, toward the divine light.

VII Hall of Saint Petronilla

The large hall is dedicated to the great painting created in 17th century Rome. The massive canvas
depicting the *Burial of Saint Petronilla* dominates
the large hall. Guercino painted it between 1621
and 1623 for an altar of the Basilica of Saint Peter.
In this painting, the artist from Cento blended
the great style derived from Caravaggio
with a perfect balance of shapes, light and
color inspired by the ideal classicism
that characterized his presumed rival,
fellow countryman Guido Reni. A
precise sequence of registers develops
with dramatic energy: below, powerful personages lower the saint into the
grave (observe the depiction of the
hands that emerge from the grave to
sustain the body in an audacious
foreshortening). Then, the visitor's
eye is directed upward where the
beautiful figure of Christ accepts
Petronilla, dressed in a rich garment,
into Heaven with an elegant gesture.
Once Guercino returned to Emilia, he
expressed a more static and more aca-
demic painting. The painting in the
center of the left wall depicting the
Persian Sibyl shows such a stylistic
change. The *Cumaean Sibyl* painted
by Domenichino is placed next to the

Persian Sibyl. Domenichino was another leader of Roman classicism inspired by Raphael.

Caravaggio, whose two extraordinary valuable canvases are on display facing the Sibyls, shifted the attention to reality. *The Good Luck* is a youthful work of art created around 1595 for the cardinal Del Monte, one of the first protectors of the artist. The subject, depicted in a painting located in the Louvre with a slightly different variation, reveals the new interest given to scenes taken from reality. The presentation of the personages painted against a clear background without any indication of environment or depth and depicted with an accurate rendering of the details is also original. *Saint John the Baptist*, painted around 1602 for the Mattei family, which numbers among the many sacred commissions, is a joyful, almost Dionysiac, moment. The way of representing the saint is revolutionary: without any religious attributes. The saint is surprised in an athletic torsion like a young shepherd. The comparison with the models taken from the past is evident (the Hellenistic sculptures and the powerful ignudi painted by Michelangelo on the vault of the Sistine Chapel). However, the use of the chiaroscuro, which exalts with live realism the figure on the indistinct background, is entirely new and particular.

The large canvas with the *Finding of Romulus and Remus*, that Rubens painted in Antwerp around 1617 constitutes a present to Rome. The prolific Flemish artist lived in the city between 1600 and 1608 and painted the splendid canvases on the apse of the Chiesa Nuova. In the painting, the central

group is derived from an ancient sculpture depicting the She-Wolf and the twins seen and drawn in the Vatican. Next to the Tiber personification, the vestal Rhea Silvia, Romulus and Remus' mother, sits on the left-hand side while Faustulus, who adopted the twins, arrives on the scene.

VIII Hall of Pietro da Cortona

This room houses a conspicuous number of the Tuscan artist's works of art. Pietro da Cortona and his school represented the main season of the Baroque, which coincided with Urban VIII's pontificate. A masterly portrait of the pope is located in the room (1626–1627). *The Rape of the Sabines* is a true indication of the new pictorial style. Indeed, in the narration of the legendary episode of the origins of Rome any stylistic symmetry is abandoned—there it was still respected in the "classical" Sacrifice of Polyxena—in favor of a dynamic and centrifugal performance that follows diagonal lines with a rapid succession of light and shade, through the sumptuous vitality of the brush-stroke.

IX Cini Gallery

The visit to the Picture Gallery ends with the long gallery that takes its name from the Roman count Francesco Cini's donation of a rich collection of porcelain (1880). The

Pieter Paul Rubens (Siegen 1577 – Antwerp 1640), *The Finding of Romulus and Remus*, detail

Pietro da Cortona (Pietro Berrettini, Cortona 1597 – Rome 1669), *Portrait of Urban VIII*

main nucleus of the collection is represented by the series of the Saxon manufacture of Meissen (18th–19th centuries): masks of the Comedy of the art, animals, the famous *Pastoral Idylls* and the original *Concert of monkeys*. Furthermore, the gallery houses several exemplars of the Italian production created in the Capodimonte factories and of Roman manufacture (1785–1818) specialized in small format replicas of famous classical sculptures (*Dying Gaul, Ares Ludovisi, Barberini Faun*), such as the prestigious biscuit of Giovanni Volpato in the immured glass case.

In the different parts of the gallery (that also houses a series of Flemish tapestries with the *stories of Semiramis*, the legendary Babylonian queen), the paintings are grouped according to genres. The types include: the landscape painting, the painting that dedicates a new interest to the daily life of the people (Cerquozzi, Salvator Rosa), and landscape, popular in the 18th century. *The Views of Rome* belong to the latter genre. Gaspar Van Wittel (1653-1736) created these tempera paintings on parchment. He was the father of the more famous architect Vanvitelli, one of the first artists who promoted in Italy the interest in the descriptive precision inherent to the north European concept of landscape.

A significant series of portraits painted between the 15 and 18th century is gathered in the next space. The works of art span from the Venetian pieces produced in the 15th century to the accentuated psychological penetration of the Bolognese artist Bartolomeo Passerotti's several canvases dating to

the first eight years of the 16th century (the *Gentleman with dog* is a magnificent example.) The intense *Portrait of a Youth* created by Giovanni Bellini stands out among the 15th century works of art. The Flemish Van Dyck's two double portraits of his artist friends, and Velázquez's *Self Portrait* disguised as a Virtuoso of the Pantheon (a congregation to which the painter belonged when he was in Rome between 1649 and 1651), instead, are exceptional testimonies of the seventeenth century portrait. Van Dyck was a portrait painter appreciated and requested by the European aristocracy. He created the double portraits when he was in Genoa around the Twenties.

The last room is dedicated to a limited amount of 18th century works of art. Domenico Corvi created the preparatory works for the tapestries of the Appartamento dei Conservatori (the Conservators' Apartment). Raphael's works inspired the artist Pompeo Batoni's *Holy Family*.

The Portrait of the cardinal Silvio Valenti Gonzaga, promoter of the creation of the Capitoline collection, painted by the French artist Pierre Subleyras, active in Rome in 1727, is placed at the end of the exhibitory route.

Diego Velázquez
(Seville 1599 – Madrid
1660), *Self Portrait*

Floor −1
Palazzo Senatorio
Tabularium

I. Gallery of the *Tabularium*
II. Hall of the Executioner
III. Temple of Veiovis
IV. Roman Staircase

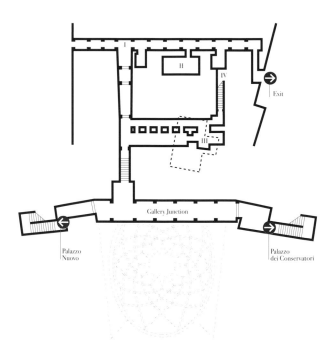

PALAZZO SENATORIO
TABULARIUM

Conjunction Gallery

Leaving the Museums, whether coming from the Palazzo Nuovo or the Palazzo dei Conservatori the visitor can descend to the subterranean level to discover the ancient buildings that once rose under the square and the Palazzo Senatorio. The excavations conducted at the end of the Thirties in the area between the base of the Marcus Aurelius statue and the building façade to build a conjunction gallery revealed the existence of an ancient road located between the *Arx* and the *Capitolium* slopes at a depth of eight meters. Large tufa blocks sustained the two slopes. The road, originating from the *Campus Martius*, turned toward the *Capitolium* running along the Temple of Vèiovis and the *Tabularium*. Brick buildings of the imperial age flanked the road. The last building had pilasters with brackets to sustain terraces.

Temple of Veiovis

After the visitors walk down a triple flight of stairs, a mysterious *genius loci* welcomes them. In fact, the *colossal cult statue of Veiovis* found, unfortunately headless, in the *cella* of the adjacent temple has been put in display here. The cult statue was carved, possibly in the Sullan age (1st century BC), from a solid block of marble. It is depicted according to a youthful iconography, almost Apollonian, found in some small bronze statues. The character of the Italic divinity has never been clear: some

The Palazzo Senatorio in the 19th century in a watercolor painting by Constant Moyaux

Facing page
The Palazzo Senatorio, section

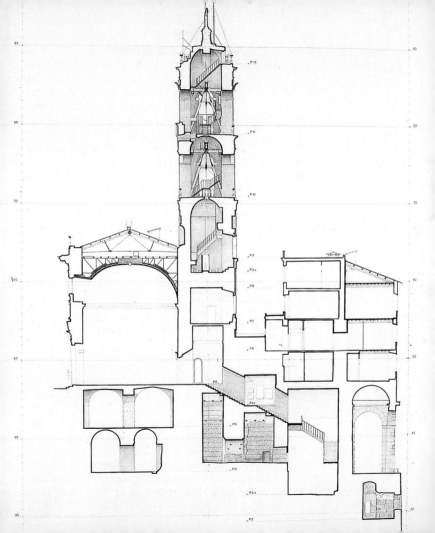

Cult statue of Veiovis

scholars think it was benign, others that it was malignant. Its relationship with Jupiter is unclear as well. Indeed, some mutual attributes (bolts of lightning and goat) and the similarity of the names (Veiovis = adolescent Jupiter) associate him with Jupiter. The remains of the sanctuary dedicated to the divinity in the Republican age are visible through two openings on the walls, protected by a glass partition. The sanctuary was built between 196 and 192 BC but it was possibly rebuilt simultaneously with the Tabularium. With an original corner built within its perimeter, the back part of the *Tabularium* respected the volumetric measures of the sanctuary to ward off ill luck. It is for this reason that the podium remained untouched on the left side and on the backside, covered in travertine panels with elegant moldings. A catwalk (which is reachable further ahead, behind the gallery facing the Forum) allows the visitors to walk above the building, which had a rectangular plan and faced west, toward the slopes of the *Capitolium*. The cella, wider than it is deep, has walls made of tufa blocks and preserves the travertine threshold. The area of the small, ancient portico with four columns, preceded by an entrance stairway along the long side, still houses an altar without inscriptions. Furthermore, near by the temple there was an internal staircase (especially well preserved) that rose from the level of the Roman Forum to the upper stores of the *Tabularium*. The construction of the podium of the Temple of Vespasian later impeded access to the travertine door entrance into the *Tabularium*.

Tabularium

An imposing structure, the premises of the ancient Roman archives, was built in the first century B.C. on the slopes facing the Roman Forum. The edifice took the name of *Tabularium* because it preserved the bronze *tabulæ* on which the laws and the official acts were engraved. Notwithstanding the importance of the architectural intervention that dramatically changed the configuration of the heart of the city (also by functioning as a structural reinforcement of the slope), no literary sources mention this building. The building was identified at the beginning of the fifteenth century through an inscription, later lost, which recorded the consul Lutatius Catulus' inspection that took place in 78 BC. The inscription is similar to the one still legible on a flat arch located in the corridor in via di San Pietro in Carcere. The construction of the *Tabularium*, therefore, could have taken place in relationship with the fire that in 83 BC destroyed the Temple of Capitoline Jupiter, restored during that magistracy. The hypothetical reconstruction of the original aspect of the building, therefore, is exclusively based on the remaining structures. However, the understanding of their original aspect is made difficult by the continuous use that they underwent. Since the Middle Ages, they housed the "salara" of the Campidoglio (a salt deposit that caused the corrosion of some walls), kitchens, stalls, and services of the Palazzo Senatorio such as the prisons for the inmates waiting to be judged and the so-called Hall of the Executioner. Today, it is difficult to understand the ancient arrangement

Reconstruction of the Temple of Veiovis

of the *Tabularium* also due to the loss of the upper stories. They were either destroyed or enveloped in new spaces when the Palazzo Senatorio was reorganized to meet the new administration needs by the creation of offices, now distinctly separated from the ancient spaces.

Currently, the Gallery is the only accessible ancient space. From it, the visitors can enjoy a marvelous view from the Colosseum to the Palatine. In the past, the Gallery was used for the public passage between the *Capitolium* and the *Arx*. Pavilion vaults covered the Gallery. One original extant example is visible in the last span closest to via San Pietro in Carcere. The Gallery is placed on a base—constructed out of opus caementicium, externally covered by enormous blocks of Gabine stone or red tufa arranged in alternate courses of "headers" and "stretchers" currently eroded by the wind—in which another much smaller gallery extends. Rectangular windows provide light to the interior of the latter gallery. The front of the upper story Doric order loggia with eleven large arches constituted a scenic background of the Roman Forum. Some of the arches were discovered only at the end of the 19th century. Some capitals made in travertine, located in the forum area at the foot of the monument, might have fallen from above and might attest to the presence of an upper floor. The aforementioned second flight of stairs near by the Temple of Vèiovis might have led to this level. Unfortunately, the stair is badly preserved. The visitor can go from the gallery to a parallel foundation space that houses interesting remains (also a beau-

tiful mosaic) of a building constructed in the 2nd century BC and destroyed for the construction of the *Tabularium*. Furthermore, in the 19th century two sections of entablatures belonging to temples in the Roman Forum were mounted on the walls of the large gallery. The section from the Temple of Concordia, reconstructed by Tiberius (beginning of the 1st century AD) presents very elegant marble engravings. The fragment found in the Temple of Vespasian and Titus (79 AD), characterized by chiaroscuro and plasticity of the reliefs, depicts in its frieze objects of cult and sacrificial instruments.

BIBLIOGRAPHY

On the preceeding pages
Roofing project
of the Roman Garden
area by Carlo
Aymonino

A. Tofanelli, *Catalogo delle sculture antiche e de' quadri esistenti nel Museo, e Gallerie di Campidoglio*, Rome 1817

P. Righetti, *Descrizione del Campidoglio*, I, Rome 1833; II, Rome 1836

A. Venturi, *La Galleria del Campidoglio*, "Archivio Storico dell'Arte", II, 1889, pp. 441-454

A. Michaelis, *Storia della collezione capitolina di antichità fino all'inaugurazione del museo* (1734), "Mitteilungen des Deutschen Archäologischen Instituts. Römische Abteilung", VI, 1891, pp. 3-66

E. Rodocanachi, *Le Capitole romain antique et moderne*, Paris 1904

R. Delbrück, *Hellenistische Bauten in Latium*, I, Strasbourg 1907, pp. 23-46, tables 3-9

H. Stuart Jones, *A Catalogue of the Ancient Sculptures preserved in the Municipal Collections of Rome. The Sculptures of the Museo Capitolino*, Oxford 1912

H. Stuart Jones, *A Catalogue of the Ancient Sculptures preserved in the Municipal Collections of Rome. The Sculptures of the Palazzo dei Conservatori*, Oxford 1926

D. Mustilli, *Il Museo Mussolini*, Rome 1939

A.M. Colini, *Aedes Veiovis*, "Bullettino della Commissione Archeologica del Governatorato di Roma", LXX, 1942, pp. 5-55

P. Pecchiai, *Il Campidoglio nel Cinquecento sulla scorta dei documenti*, Rome 1950

C. Pietrangeli, *Nuovi lavori nella più antica pinacoteca di Roma*, "Capitolium", XXVI, 1951, pp. 59-71

R. Righetti, *Gemme e cammei delle collezioni comunali*, Rome 1955

(Various authors), *Il Campidoglio*, "Capitolium", XXXIX, 4, 1964

(Various authors), *Il colle capitolino e l'Ara Coeli*, "Capitolium", XL, 4, 1965

G. De Angelis D'Ossat, C. Pietrangeli, *Il Campidoglio di Michelangelo*, Milan 1965

W. Helbig, *Führer durch die öffentlichen Sammlungen klassischer Altertümer in Rom*, II, Tübingen 1966[4]

C. D'Onofrio, *Renovatio Romae*, Rome 1973

C. Pietrangeli (editor), *Musei Capitolini. Guida Breve*, Rome 1974[8]

R. Bruno, *Pinacoteca Capitolina*, Bologna 1978

C. Pietrangeli (editor), *Guida del Campidoglio* (Guide rionali di Roma, Rione X – Campitelli, parte II), Rome 1983[3]

E. La Rocca, M.E. Tittoni, *Musei Capitolini*, Milan 1984

M. Cima, E. La Rocca (editors), *Le tranquille dimore degli dei*, exhibition catalogue (Rome 1986), Venice 1986

Da Pisanello alla nascita dei Musei Capitolini, exhibition catalogue (Rome 1988), Milan 1988

M.E. Tittoni, *La Buona Ventura del Caravaggio: note e precisazioni in margine al restauro*, "Quaderni di Palazzo Venezia", 1989, 6, pp. 179-184

Identificazione di un Caravaggio, Venice 1990

Il tesoro di via Alessandrina, exhibition catalogue (Rome 1990), Rome 1990

Il Campidoglio e Sisto V, exhibition catalogue (Rome 1991), Rome 1991

Guercino e le collezioni capitoline, exhibition catalogue (Rome 1991), Rome 1991

Ch. Reusser, *Der Fidestempel auf dem Kapitol in Rom und seine Ausstattung*, Rome 1993

J. Bentini (editor), *Quadri rinomatissimi: il collezionismo dei Pio di Savoia*, Modena 1994

(Various authors), *La facciata del Palazzo Senatorio in Campidoglio. Momenti di storia urbana in Roma*, Pisa 1994

A. Mura Sommella, *Contributo allo studio del* Tabularium

attraverso l'analisi di alcuni documenti iconografici e d'archivio relativi al Palazzo Senatorio, "Palladio", n.s. VII, 14, 1994, pp. 45-54

La natura morta al tempo di Caravaggio, exhibition catalogue (Rome 1995-1996), Naples 1995

(Various authors), La facciata del Palazzo Senatorio in Campidoglio. Momenti di un grande restauro a Roma, Pisa 1995

E. La Rocca, Prima del Palazzo Senatorio: i monumenti inter duos lucos, in (Various authors), La facciata del Palazzo Senatorio in Campidoglio. Momenti di un grande restauro a Roma, op. cit., pp. 15-30

(Various authors), Il Palazzo dei Conservatori e il Palazzo Nuovo in Campidoglio. Momenti

di storia urbana in Roma, Pisa 1996

Classicismo e natura – La lezione di Domenichino, exhibition catalogue (Rome 1996-1997), Milan 1996

(Various authors), Il Palazzo dei Conservatori e il Palazzo Nuovo in Campidoglio. Momenti di un grande restauro a Roma, Pisa 1997

Pietro da Cortona, il meccanismo della forma, exhibition catalogue (Rome 1997-1998), Milan 1997

Il Seicento a Roma – Da Caravaggio a Salvator Rosa, exhibition catalogue (Milan 1999), Milan 1999

Caravaggio's "St. John" & Masterpieces from the Capitoline Museum in Rome, exhibition catalogue (Hartford-Toronto 1999), Hartford 1999

M. Bertoletti, M. Cima, E. Talamo (editors), Sculptures of Ancient Rome. The Collections of the Capitoline Museums at the Montemartini Power Plant, Milan 1999²

M.E. Tittoni, Pinacoteca Capitolina praticamente nuova, "Capitolium Millennio", III, 1999, 11-12, pp. 67-70

(Various authors), The Capitoline Museums, Milan 2000

La Lupa Capitolina, exhibition catalogue (Rome 2000), Milan 2000